Ice Cream Cookbook

Easy and Healthy Recipes of Fresh Homemade Ice Creams, Sorbet, Ice Pops Recipes for You and Your Family

Wendy Wood

Legal & Disclaimer

The information contained in this book and its contents is not designed to replace or take the place of any form of medical or professional advice; and is not meant to replace the need for independent medical, financial, legal or other professional advice or services, as may be required. The content and information in this book have been provided for educational and entertainment purposes only.

The content and information contained in this book have been compiled from sources deemed reliable, and it is accurate to the best of the Author's knowledge, information, and belief. However, the Author cannot guarantee its accuracy and validity and cannot be held liable for any errors and/or omissions. Further, changes are periodically made to this book as and when needed. Where appropriate and/or necessary, you must consult a professional (including but not limited to your doctor, attorney, financial advisor or such other professional advisor) before using any of the suggested remedies, techniques, or information in this book.

Upon using the contents and information contained in this book, you agree to hold harmless the Author from and against any damages, costs, and expenses, including any legal fees potentially resulting from the application of any of the information provided by this book. This disclaimer applies to any loss, damages or injury caused by the use and application, whether directly or indirectly, of any advice or information presented, whether for breach of contract, tort, negligence, personal injury, criminal intent, or under any other cause of action.

You agree to accept all risks of using the information presented in this book.
You agree that by continuing to read this book, where appropriate and/or necessary, you shall consult a professional (including but not limited to your doctor, attorney, or financial advisor or such other advisor as needed) before using any of the suggested remedies, techniques, or information in this book.

Table of Contents

Introduction

Sorbet is an icy, fresh and delicious summer dessert that is loved by both adults and children. This cold dessert is great for people who are adherents of a healthy diet and follow strict diets, as well as for people who want to enjoy the taste of natural berries and fruits. It is low in calories and contains natural juices and purees. When making sorbet, you can use honey or maple syrup instead of sugar. In this dessert, a sweetener is used to a minimum, since fruits and berries have enough natural sweetness and therefore the sorbet comes out so refreshing and not sugary. To make the sorbet taste original, you can replace fruit puree with vegetable one - for example, tomato sorbet, celery sorbet, cucumber-basil sorbet can be served as an appetizer for lunch and this is unusual and healthy.

This fruit and berry dessert has a light cool texture and a high concentration of glucose, it is dietary, it is low in calories and high in vitamins, because it is prepared from fresh berries and fruits that can be frozen beforehand. And as we know, glucose is the main source of energy. It enters the bloodstream and is carried throughout the body, providing the energy necessary for the metabolic process. Our brain works continuously 24 hours a day and glucose is vital for normal human mental activity. Of course, everything should be in moderation. If you have any kind of allergy to any berries or fruits, then it is better to consult your doctor or replace in the recipe for those berries to which you are not allergic.

Historically, this cold dessert ranks first among ice desserts, as it was invented long before ice cream appeared. Sorbet resembles soft popsicles, in fact it is, but only without cream. Sorbet can be served not only at the end of dinner, but also before serving hot dishes, as it refreshes, especially citrus fruits, because they are not very sweet and improves digestion. The recipe is quite simple, although it takes a long freeze from 3 to 12 hours, and in order to achieve a uniform consistency, the sorbet should be mixed several times during the entire freezing time.

Ice cream is the same delicious summer and cold dessert that will bring a little coolness on hot days, but it is creamier than sorbet because it contains milk, cream or yogurt. The history of ice cream goes back thousands of years; back in ancient China, it was served in the form of crushed ice with fruits and berries.

You can also replace sugar with honey or maple syrup, and if you are allergic to animal milk, you can replace it with plant milk such as coconut, almond, rice, oatmeal, poppy seed, soy. But still, be sure to consult with your doctor in order not to harm yourself.

As you know, milk is rich in calcium and by consuming ice cream in moderate doses, you will saturate your body with minerals, vitamins, amino acids, as well as calcium. The composition of ice cream contains berries and fruits, which are also very useful and contain many vitamins and antioxidants.

We all come from childhood and as adults we want pleasant memories and emotions, and a delicious delicacy such as ice cream gives us these wonderful memories. It turns out that the composition of the milk dessert contains the useful amino acid L-tryptophan, which has antidepressant properties. This substance is involved in a reaction that leads to the formation of the hormone of joy - serotonin, it improves our mood and reduces stress. It helps you cope with stress, makes you feel good, and even improves your memory.

I bring to your attention 55 delicious summer sorbet and ice cream recipes that will delight you on hot summer days. The composition of the ingredients can vary depending on your wishes. In any case, you need a blender, just a little patience and a good mood!

Sorbet

Spicy Berry Sorbet

Servings: 4
Cooking Time: 15 minutes

INGREDIENTS:

- Frozen raspberries 140 g
- Frozen pitted cherries 280 g
- Mint leaves 15 g
- Cinnamon ½ tsp.
- Nutmeg ¼ tsp
- Vanilla sugar ½ tsp.

DIRECTIONS:

1. Remove the berries from the freezer and leave them warm for 15 minutes. Finely chop the mint, add it to the berries, grind the mixture in a blender or juicer with a sorbet attachment. Add spices and sugar to taste, mix thoroughly. You can serve immediately.

   Enjoy your meal.

Strawberry Sorbet

Servings: 6
Cooking Time: 3 hours

INGREDIENTS:

- Fresh strawberries 300 g
- Sugar 100 g
- Lemon ½
- Water 50 ml

DIRECTIONS:

1. Dissolve sugar in water over low heat and cook until bubbles begin to appear on the surface. Remove the pan from heat. Let the liquid cool.
2. Cut the strawberries into small wedges, drizzle with lemon juice and leave for a few minutes to absorb the juice.
3. Grind the strawberries in a blender, mix with the chilled syrup, and place them in the freezer for 3 hours. Stir every 30 minutes to avoid ice lumps. Serve the sorbet with berry wedges.

Enjoy your meal!

Watermelon Sorbet

Servings: 2
Cooking Time: 2 hours

INGREDIENTS:

- Watermelon 250 gr
- Lemon 0.5 lemon
- A couple of mint leaves
- Water 25 ml

DIRECTIONS:

1. Pour boiling water over the mint and let it brew.
2. Remove the seeds from the watermelon, and grind the watermelon in a blender. Then add lemon juice and mint. Beat again in a blender, then transfer to a container and send to the freezer for 2 hours.

   Enjoy your meal!

Apple Sorbet

Servings: 2
Cooking Time: 4 hours

INGREDIENTS:

- Lemon ½ pc.
- Apple 2 pcs.
- Sugar 1.5 tbsp. l
- Apricot jam 1.5 tsp
- Brandy 5 tbsp

DIRECTIONS:

1. Dice the apples and mix in a blender with apricot jam, sugar, lemon juice, and brandy until smooth.
2. Pass the puree through a sieve and put in the freezer for 4 hours, stirring occasionally, until it cools completely.

Enjoy your meal!

Mango Sorbet

Servings: 2
Cooking Time: 3 hours

INGREDIENTS:

- Water 5 tbsp. l
- Sugar 4.5 tbsp. l
- Mango 1 pc
- Lemon ½ pc

DIRECTIONS:

1. Prepare the syrup, bring the water and sugar to a boil, stirring to dissolve the sugar completely. Remove from heat and cool.
2. Grind the mango in a blender and pass through a sieve, then combine with syrup and lemon juice.
3. Put the puree in a container and put it in the freezer for 3 hours and stir periodically to break the ice crystals.

Enjoy your meal!

Kiwi Sorbet With Mint

Servings: 2
Cooking Time: 3 hours

INGREDIENTS:

- Water 4 tbsp. l
- Sugar 2.5 tbsp. l
- Kiwi 4 pcs
- Lemon juice to taste
- Mint to taste

DIRECTIONS:

1. Pour sugar into boiling water and cook for 5 minutes until thick syrup, then remove and cool.
2. Pass the peeled kiwi through a sieve and mix with sugar syrup and lemon juice. We put it in the freezer for 1 hour.
3. Remove and stir in a blender or whisk and put the sorbet in the refrigerator for another 2 hours.

Enjoy your meal!

Banana-Citrus Sorbet

Servings: 2
Cooking Time: 6 hours

INGREDIENTS:

- Lemon 100 g
- Banana 1 pc
- Oranges 50 g
- Sugar 2 tbsp. l
- Apple juice 2.5 tbsp l

DIRECTIONS:

1. Peel the lemon and orange from the peel and seeds
2. Place the peeled banana and citrus ingredients in a blender bowl.
3. Then add the apple juice with sugar and mix again in a blender.
4. Freeze sorbet in the freezer for 6 hours, stirring 2-3 times.

Enjoy your meal!

Lemon-Lime Sorbet

Servings: 2
Cooking Time: 4 hours

INGREDIENTS:

- Lemon 1.5 pcs
- Lime 1 pc
- Sugar 4.5 tbsp. l
- Mineral water with gas 4 tbsp. l
- Fresh mint for garnish

DIRECTIONS:

1. Remove the zest from the lime with a fine grater and squeeze the juice from the lemon and lime to make a glass.
2. Add sugar to the juice and heat until the sugar is completely dissolved, then cool the syrup.
3. Transfer to a freezer container, add lime zest, and stir. Add sparkling water gradually and taste it. Put in the freezer for 3-4 hours, stirring every 30-40 minutes. Garnish with mint when serving.

Enjoy your meal!

Melon Sorbet With Chopped Mint

Servings: 2
Cooking Time: 2 hours

INGREDIENTS:

- Melon 250 g
- Glucose syrup 50 g
- Lemon juice 25 ml
- Mint 4 g

DIRECTIONS:

1. Peel the melon and bring the pulp to a puree consistency.
2. In a saucepan, combine glucose syrup and melon puree and bring to a boil, then add lemon juice, chopped mint, and cool.
3. We place it in a container and put it in the freezer for 2 hours, then form balls and serve.
   Enjoy your meal!

Banana-Apricot Sorbet

Servings: 2
Cooking Time: 12 hours

INGREDIENTS:

- Bananas 2 piece
- Apricot 300g
- Water 150ml
- Sugar 30g

DIRECTIONS:

1. In a saucepan, bring water and sugar to a boil.
2. Peel the bananas, remove the pits from the apricots, mix in a blender until smooth and add the cooled syrup, and then mix again.
3. Transfer the puree to a container and put it in the freezer for 12 hours.
4. After 12 hours, remove the mixture from the freezer and mix again in the blender. Transfer it to a container and put it back in the freezer for better consistency.
5. Spoon the finished sorbet into beautiful bowls and serve, garnished with mint leaves.

Enjoy your meal!

Orange Sorbet

Servings: 2
Cooking Time: 2 hours

INGREDIENTS:

- Orange 3 pcs
- Lemon 1/2
- Sugar 70 g
- Water 100 g

DIRECTIONS:

1. Cut the oranges in half and carefully remove the pulp. Place the peel in the refrigerator to cool.
2. In a saucepan, combine water and sugar and cook until syrup forms. We cool it down.
3. Squeeze juice from the pulp of oranges and half a lemon and add to the chilled syrup, mix. We fold it into a mold and put it in the freezer for 2 hours, during this time we take it out and mix it 2-3 times.
4. Place the sorbet in the chilled orange zest halves.

Enjoy your meal!

Vanilla Sorbet With Blueberries

Servings: 3
Cooking Time: 3 hours

INGREDIENTS:

- Milk (we recommend coconut) 300 ml
- Vanilla extract 1 tsp
- Blueberries 90 g
- Sugar 5 tbsp. l

DIRECTIONS:

1. In a blender, beat half the milk with sugar and vanilla for 5-7 minutes. Pour into molds so that the milk mixture is half full. We put it in the freezer for an hour.
2. Next, beat the remaining milk with blueberries in a blender for 5-7 minutes. Pour the finished blueberry milk base into the empty places in the tins and place in the freezer for 5 hours.

Enjoy your meal!

Blueberry Sorbet

Servings: 2
Cooking Time: 3 hours

INGREDIENTS:

- Blueberries 3 cups
- Sugar ½ cup
- 1/2 cup water
- Lemon juice 1 tbsp l

DIRECTIONS:

1. In a saucepan, combine water with sugar and cook until it is completely dissolved, then remove from heat and cool.
2. We interrupt the washed blueberries in a blender until smooth and then combine them with chilled syrup and lemon juice.
3. We transfer the finished consistency to a container and put it in the freezer for at least 3 hours, taking it out every 30 minutes and stirring it with a whisk.

Enjoy your meal!

Currant Sorbet

Servings: 3
Cooking Time: 2 hours

INGREDIENTS:

- Red currant - 450 g
- Powdered sugar - 150 g
- Water - 110 ml

DIRECTIONS:

1. Freeze the currants a little, pour in a little water, and interrupt in a blender, add the remaining water and add powdered sugar, mix. Transfer to a convenient container and place in the freezer. Stir every hour. Serve to the table in nice wide glasses.

   Enjoy your meal!

Apricot Sorbet

Servings: 3
Cooking Time: 3,5 hours

INGREDIENTS:

- Apricots - 700 g
- Sugar - 230 g
- Water - 230 ml
- Vanilla extract - to taste

DIRECTIONS:

1. Peel the apricots, fill with water and cook for 10 minutes.
2. Remove from heat and add sugar, stir and leave to cool. Grind the cooled mixture in a blender. Then add vanilla extract. We transfer the puree to a container and put it in the freezer, after half an hour you need to get it out and again interrupt in a blender. Then we take out and mix every hour.
3. Serve to the table in nice wide glasses.

Enjoy your meal!

Cherry Sorbet

Servings: 4
Cooking Time: 3 hours

INGREDIENTS:

- Frozen cherries 1.5 kg
- Sugar 200 gr
- Lemon 0.5
- Water 3 tbsp. l

DIRECTIONS:

1. You need to get the cherries out of the freezer, it is imperative that they are pitted and let them defrost a little.
2. We make the syrup: mix the water with sugar and add half of the lemon juice, cook the syrup over low heat, stirring until the sugar is completely dissolved, let it cool. Grind the cherries and syrup in a blender, transfer them to a container and send them to the freezer. Stir every hour.
3. Serve to the table in nice wide glasses.

Enjoy your meal!

Sorbet With Raspberries And Blueberries

Servings: 6
Cooking Time: 3 hours

INGREDIENTS:

- Raspberries 300 g
- Blueberries 600 g
- Sugar 300 g
- Lemon 0.5

DIRECTIONS:

1. Combine the berries with lemon juice and sugar, begin to beat until smooth in a blender. We transfer it to a container and put it in the freezer, stir periodically so that there are no pieces of ice.
2. Serve to the table in nice wide glasses.

Enjoy your meal!

Raspberry Sorbet

Servings: 2
Cooking Time: 3 hours

INGREDIENTS:

- Fresh raspberries - 200 g
- Granulated sugar - 100-150 g
- Milk - 100 ml
- Mint - for serving

DIRECTIONS:

1. We wash the raspberries and combine with sugar, knead with a fork and let the sugar completely dissolve in 15-20 minutes. Add milk and mix well. Pour into a container and place in the freezer, stirring occasionally to avoid ice crystals, and garnish with mint leaves when serving.

   Enjoy your meal!

Berry Sorbet With Sea Buckthorn

Servings: 4
Cooking Time: 3 hours

INGREDIENTS:

- Sea buckthorn - 180 g
- Blueberries - 230 g
- Orange - ½ pc.
- Orange peel - 1 tbsp. l.
- Syrup (of your choice) - 50 ml

DIRECTIONS:

1. We wash all the berries and wipe them. Rub the orange zest on a fine grater. In a blender, mix blueberries, sea buckthorn, orange pulp, zest, and syrup. We transfer to a container and put it in the freezer for 3 hours, stirring occasionally.

   Enjoy your meal!

Apple Cranberry Sorbet

Servings: 4
Cooking Time: 6 hours

INGREDIENTS:

- Apple 3 pcs.
- Cranberries 1.5 glass.
- Filtered water 150 ml.
- Sugar 100 g.
- Several mint leaves.

DIRECTIONS:

1. Pour sugar into boiling water and boil stirring for 8 minutes until sugar is completely dissolved. Then leave the syrup to cool. Peel and seed apples, cut into pieces, and beat in a blender until smooth. Add cranberries and chilled syrup and beat together in a blender. Transfer to a container and place in the freezer for 6 hours, stirring occasionally. Garnish with mint when serving.

Enjoy your meal!

Plum Sorbet

Servings: 8
Cooking Time: 4-6 hours

INGREDIENTS:

- Plums 600 g
- Sugar 150 g
- Lemon juice 4 tbsp l.
- Water 100 ml
- A pinch of salt

DIRECTIONS:

1. We take out the seeds from the ripe plums and cut them into slices. Put all the ingredients in boiling water and cook for 15-17 minutes to soften the plums. Then let it cool. Whisk the cooled syrup with plums in a blender, then grind through a fine sieve and transfer to a container, and put in the freezer for 4 hours, periodically stir until completely frozen.

   Enjoy your meal!

Pineapple Sorbet

Servings: 4
Cooking Time: 6 hours

INGREDIENTS:

- Pineapple 600 g
- Banana 1 pc
- Sugar 0.5 tbsp. l

DIRECTIONS:

1. Ripe pineapple, peel, and core, cut into large slices. We put all the ingredients in a blender and grind well. Transfer the finished puree to a container and put it in the freezer for 6 hours. After an hour, the sorbet needs to be stirred and put back in the freezer.

   Enjoy your meal!

Strawberry Banana Sorbet

Servings: 2
Cooking Time: 1 hours

INGREDIENTS:

- Frozen strawberries 3.5 tbsp
- Bananas 2 pcs
- Sugar or honey to taste

DIRECTIONS:

1. Cut strongly frozen bananas and strawberries into pieces, add sugar (honey) and mix in a blender until smooth. Can be left in the refrigerator for an hour or immediately served.

   Enjoy your meal!

Peach Sorbet

Servings: 3
Cooking Time: 3 hours

INGREDIENTS:

- Peaches 5 (ripe)
- Sugar ¾ tbsp.
- Water ¾ tbsp.
- Lemon juice 1 tsp
- A pinch of salt

DIRECTIONS:

1. It is necessary to peel the peaches, cut them into slices and freeze a little. Dissolve the sugar in water, add lemon juice, salt, and frozen peaches and grind very well in a blender until smooth. We transfer the mashed potatoes to a container and put them in the freezer for 3 hours, stirring occasionally.

   Enjoy your meal!

Strawberry Sorbet With Basil

Servings: 4
Cooking Time: 4 hours

INGREDIENTS:

- Strawberries 600 g
- Powdered sugar 60 g
- Juice of half a lemon
- Basil green 8 large leaves

DIRECTIONS:

1. Wash the strawberries and cool slightly in the refrigerator. Grind the strawberries in a blender, then add the powdered sugar, basil, lemon juice and grind very well again. Then pour the puree into a container and place in the freezer for 4 hours, stirring occasionally.

   Enjoy your meal!

Black Grape Sorbet

Servings: 5
Cooking Time: 3 hours

INGREDIENTS:

- Grapes (frozen) 500 g
- Sugar 70 g
- Lemon juice 2 tbsp

DIRECTIONS:

1. Wash the grapes and refrigerate a little. Then add sugar and grind in a blender, if necessary, filter through a sieve to remove the bones. Mix the finished puree with lemon juice. Fill the container and put it in the freezer for 3 hours, stirring occasionally.

   Enjoy your meal!

Pear And Blackberry Sorbet

Servings: 6
Cooking Time: 3 hours

INGREDIENTS:

- Pears 4 pcs
- Frozen blackberries 2 tbsp
- Sugar 12 tbsp l
- Water 10 tbsp. l
- Lemon juice 4 tbsp l

DIRECTIONS:

1. Place the blackberries out of the freezer to melt a little.
2. Prepare the syrup: add sugar to the water and cook until the sugar is completely dissolved. Add the chopped pears to the syrup and cook for another 10-15 minutes to soften the pears. Add blackberries to the syrup and turn off after 2 minutes, add lemon juice and let the syrup cool.
3. Whisk everything in a blender, transfer to a container, and place in the freezer, stirring occasionally.

Enjoy your meal!

Blackberry Sorbet

Servings: 8
Cooking Time: 6 hours

INGREDIENTS:

- Blackberries 700 g
- Sugar 200 g
- Water 170 ml
- Lemon juice 2 tbsp

DIRECTIONS:

1. Cooking syrup: mix water and sugar and bring to a boil, cook over low heat, stirring occasionally, until sugar is completely dissolved. Cool the syrup and refrigerate.
2. Pour blackberries with cold syrup and grind well in a blender. Wipe the berry mass through a sieve, add lemon juice, mix and transfer to a container. We put it in the freezer and stir periodically (every hour).

Enjoy your meal!

Cucumber-Basil Sorbet

Servings: 4
Cooking Time: 3 hours

INGREDIENTS:

- Cucumber 250 g
- Honey (or maple syrup) 4 tbsp l.
- Basil 15 g
- Rum (optional) 0.5 tbsp l.

DIRECTIONS:

1. It is necessary to put all the ingredients in a blender and grind everything until smooth. Then put the puree in a container and put it in the freezer. When the sorbet is frozen, you can grind it again in a blender and serve.

Enjoy your meal!

Beetroot Sorbet

Servings: 3
Cooking Time: 5 hours

INGREDIENTS:

- Beets - 1 pc. (150-200 g)
- Honey - 50 g
- Water - 80 ml
- Orange - 1 pc.
- Lemon juice - 2 tsp.

DIRECTIONS:

1. We bake the beets in the oven at 200 °C for 1 hour. Cool, peel, and cut into large cubes. Cooking syrup: mix water and sugar and bring to a boil, cook over low heat, stirring occasionally, until sugar is completely dissolved. After you need to cool the syrup. Put the beets in a blender, add orange juice and lemon juice and grind well. Add syrup and mix. We transfer to a container and put it in the freezer, stirring occasionally.

   Enjoy your meal!

Ice Cream

Apricot Ice Cream

Servings: 2
Cooking Time: no freeze

INGREDIENTS:

- Apricot 200 g
- Banana 1 pc
- Milk 50 ml
- Brown sugar 1 tbsp

DIRECTIONS:

1. Wash the apricots, remove the seeds and send them to the freezer for 1-2 hours. Peel bananas and cut into large pieces, also freeze for 1-2 hours.
2. Grind frozen bananas in a blender and add frozen apricots there and bring to a homogeneous mass.
3. Add cold milk and brown sugar to a blender, stir, place on bowls and serve, garnish with mint.
4. Re-freezing is not required, otherwise, the ice cream will turn into ice.

Enjoy your meal!

Orange Ice Cream

Servings: 2
Cooking Time: 2 hours

INGREDIENTS:

- Milk 500 ml
- Cream 300 ml
- Sugar 200 gr
- Oranges 1 pc
- Water 50 ml

DIRECTIONS:

1. Remove the zest from a pure orange on a fine grater, squeeze the juice from the orange. Pour sugar, zest into a saucepan with a thick bottom, pour in juice and a little water. Cook the mixture over low heat until the sugar is completely dissolved, then cool the syrup and add cream and milk to it, mix thoroughly.
2. Cool in the refrigerator, then put in the freezer and after half an hour until soft, beat with a mixer, repeating this procedure every 30 minutes 4 more times.

Enjoy your meal!

Chocolate Ice Cream

Servings: 2
Cooking Time: 3 hours

INGREDIENTS:

- Dark chocolate 50 gr
- Sugar 1.5 tbsp
- Cream (35%) 150 ml
- Milk 65 ml

DIRECTIONS:

1. Combine milk and sugar in a saucepan and bring to a boil, stirring occasionally. Remove from heat and cool slightly, add chocolate, breaking it into pieces, and mix thoroughly, you should get a homogeneous mass. We set to cool. Gently beat the cream and gradually add to the chocolate mass, you should get a fluffy mass,
2. Place in a mold and place in the freezer for 3 hours.
3. During this time, stir 3-4 times with a fork so that there are no ice crystals. As it thickens, the ice cream is ready.

Enjoy your meal!

Raspberry Ice Cream

Servings: 2
Cooking Time: 3 hours

INGREDIENTS:

- Raspberries - 250 g
- Cream (at least 30% fat) - 250 ml.
- Sugar - 100 g
- Vanilla sugar - 1 sachet
- Lemon juice - 1 tbsp. l

DIRECTIONS:

1. Rub the raspberries through a sieve and add lemon juice, sugar, and stir until the sugar is completely dissolved. We put the finished consistency in the freezer for 10 minutes.
2. Whip the cream with vanilla sugar until a strong foam and add to the raspberry puree, mix gently until smooth. We put it in the freezer for 2 hours. We take out, mix, and leave again for 1 hour.

Enjoy your meal!

Ice Cream With Kiwi

Servings: 2
Cooking Time: 2 hours

INGREDIENTS:

- Kiwi 2 pcs
- Condensed milk 200 g
- Yogurt 200 g

DIRECTIONS:

1. Cut the peeled kiwi into pieces and put in a blender, beat until smooth, add condensed milk and yogurt, beat everything well until the consistency of thick sour cream.
2. Pour into glasses and insert wooden sticks inside.
3. We put the forms in the freezer for 2 hours. We take out and lower the molds for a couple of seconds into a container with hot water to make it easier to get the ice cream out of the molds.

Enjoy your meal!

Blackcurrant And Yogurt Ice Cream

Servings: 2
Cooking Time: 3 hours

INGREDIENTS:

- Frozen black currant 350 g
- Natural yogurt 250 g
- Ripe banana 1pc
- Honey 50 g

DIRECTIONS:

1. Place the currants in a saucepan and bring to a boil, cook over low heat for 5 minutes until the berries become very soft.
2. Peel the banana, cut it into cubes and grind it together with honey in a blender. Add the cooled currants to the banana and grind again in a blender until smooth. Add yogurt and beat again.
3. Pour the finished puree into cups and insert wooden sticks. We put it in the freezer for 3 hours.

Enjoy your meal!

Carrot Ice Cream

Servings: 2
Cooking Time: 12 hours

INGREDIENTS:

- Carrots (boiled) 1 pc.
- Sugar 1 tbsp
- Fat cream 100 g
- Condensed milk 50 g
- Vanilla sugar 1 packet

DIRECTIONS:

1. Peel the carrots, cut into large cubes, boil until tender, drain the water.
2. Add sugar, vanilla sugar to hot carrot puree and beat.
3. Transfer the puree to a bowl, add cream, condensed milk and beat well with a mixer, starting at low speed and ending at maximum speed.
4. Transfer to a container, close the lid tightly and place in the freezer for 12 hours.

Enjoy your meal!

Curd Ice Cream

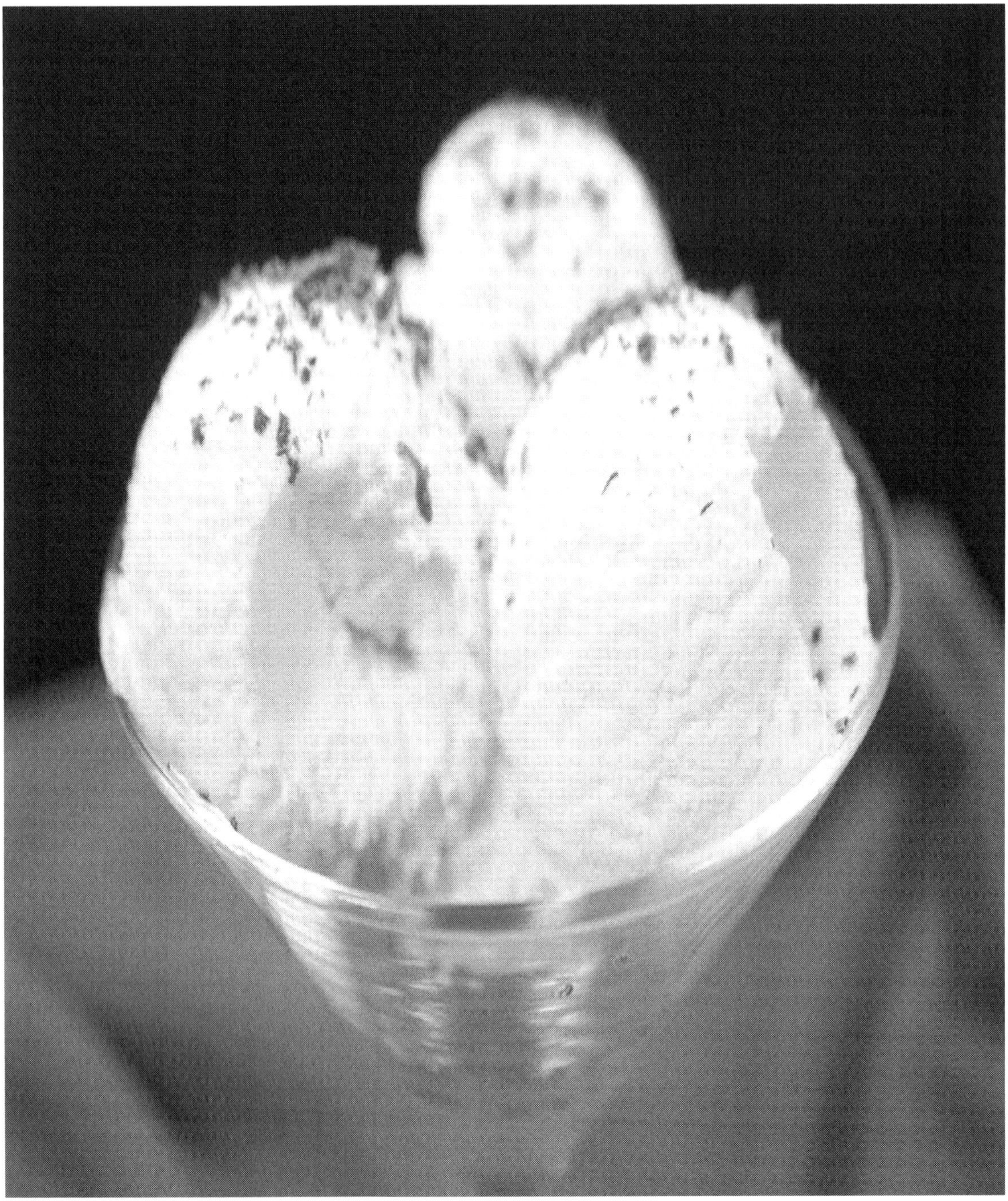

Servings: 2
Cooking Time: 3 hours

INGREDIENTS:

- Strawberry 150g
- Bananas 1pc
- Liquid honey 1 tbsp. l
- Curd 150 g

DIRECTIONS:

1. We interrupt the cottage cheese and strawberries in a blender. If the berry is frozen, then you can defrost it a little.
2. Peel the banana, add to a blender and chop until smooth. Add honey and grind again for a second.
3. Pour the mixture into a container and place in the freezer for 3 hours. Be sure to stir every 30 minutes to prevent ice cream from turning into ice.

Enjoy your meal!

Sea Buckthorn Ice Cream

Servings: 2
Cooking Time: 4-6 hours

INGREDIENTS:

- Sea buckthorn - 350 g
- Cream - 150 ml (33% fat)
- Sugar - 60 g

DIRECTIONS:

1. We interrupt the sea buckthorn in a blender and rub the finished puree through a sieve from the seeds.
2. Add cream and sugar and mix thoroughly.
3. Pour into ice cream tins and place in the freezer for 4-6 hours.

Enjoy your meal!

Strawberry Ice Cream

Servings: 2
Cooking Time: 4-5 hours

INGREDIENTS:

- strawberry 250 g
- condensed milk 150 g
- cream (from 33% fat) 125g
- vanilla sugar - 0.5 tsp.

DIRECTIONS:

1. Wash the strawberries thoroughly. Transfer to a blender and beat until smooth. Rub the puree through a fine sieve so that there are no bones. Pour the condensed milk into the mixture and beat until smooth.
2. Combine cream with vanilla sugar in a separate bowl, beat with a mixer until heavy cream is formed. Then add whipped cream in small portions to the strawberry puree and mix thoroughly.
3. Transfer the finished mixture to a container, close the lid and put it in the freezer for 4-5 hours.
4. The first 2 hours can be taken out and mixed, although due to the composition of the ice cream, there will be practically no ice crystals.

Enjoy your meal!

Mango Ice Cream

Servings: 2
Cooking Time: 2 hours

INGREDIENTS:

- Mango - 400 g
- Yogurt 2.5% - 200 g
- Mint - 5 leaves
- Honey - 2 tablespoons

DIRECTIONS:

1. Peel the mango and freeze it in cubes. Put the frozen mango in a blender and add the yogurt, mint and honey (or wedge syrup) and mix well again. Can be served immediately or placed in the freezer, stirring every hour for 4 hours.

   Enjoy your meal!

Avocado And Arugula Ice Cream

Servings: 2
Cooking Time: 2 hours

INGREDIENTS:

- Avocado - 1 pc.
- Fresh arugula - 30 g
- Banana - 1 pc.
- Lime - 1 pc.
- Maple syrup - to taste

DIRECTIONS:

1. Peel the avocado, remove the pit, peel the banana, wash the arugula and lime (squeeze the juice). We send everything to a blender and grind. We put it in a container and put it in the freezer for 2 hours. Stir every 30 minutes. Drizzle with maple syrup when serving

   Enjoy your meal!

Blueberry Ice Cream

Servings: 4
Cooking Time: 4 hours

INGREDIENTS:

- Blueberries - 200 g
- Milk - 600 ml
- Whipped cream - 100 g
- Sugar - 100 g
- Starch - 20 g

DIRECTIONS:

1. Wash and grind blueberries in a blender. Add milk and heat, add starch as it warms up. Stir constantly until the mixture is like a liquid jelly in consistency. Cool the finished mixture, then add the whipped cream to it and stir with a spatula until smooth. Transfer to a container and place in the freezer for 4 hours, stirring occasionally to avoid ice crystals. Ice cream is ready.

Enjoy your meal!

Avocado Ice Cream

Servings: 2
Cooking Time: 2 hours

INGREDIENTS:

- Ripe avocado 2 pcs
- Banana 1.5 pcs
- Milk 250 ml
- Lemon or lime juice 1 tbsp
- Honey or maple syrup 2 tablespoons

DIRECTIONS:

1. Peel the avocado, remove the pit. Peel the banana. We send to a blender and grind, add lemon or lime juice and mix well. Add honey or maple syrup, then add milk and stir well. Transfer to a container and leave in the freezer for 2 hours, stirring every 30 minutes.

   Enjoy your meal!

Banana Ice Cream

Servings: 4
Cooking Time: 2 hours

INGREDIENTS:

- Banana 3 pcs.
- Cream 10-20% 100 ml
- Icing sugar 1 tablespoon
- Lemon juice 1 tablespoon

DIRECTIONS:

1. Cut the bananas into pieces and freeze for 3-4 hours. Put frozen bananas in a blender and grind until smooth. Add cream, icing sugar and lemon juice and beat again. We transfer to a container and put in the freezer for 2 hours, stirring every 30 minutes

   Enjoy your meal!

Avocado And Lemon Ice Cream

Servings: 2
Cooking Time: 5 hours

INGREDIENTS:

- Avocado 2 pcs
- Honey 150 g
- Lemon / lime 2 pcs

DIRECTIONS:

1. Peel the avocado. You need to remove the bone. Squeeze out the lemon / lime juice and transfer everything to a blender. We put it in a container and put it in the freezer for 5 hours. Stir every 30 minutes.

   Enjoy your meal!

Lemon Ice Cream

Servings: 2
Cooking Time: 4 hours

INGREDIENTS:

- Cream 30-33% 550 g
- Sugar 150 g
- Lemon juice 70 ml - 1 pc.
- Zest (1 lemon)
- Yolk 3 pcs.
- Vanilla sugar 1 teaspoon

DIRECTIONS:

1. Place yolks, lemon juice and zest, sugar and vanilla sugar in a bowl. Stir well with a whisk. Pour into a saucepan and cook until thickened over low heat, stirring occasionally. Remove from heat and cool. Beat the cream with a mixer until thickened.
2. Pour the cooled egg mixture into the cream and stir well with a spatula. We transfer to a container and put in the freezer for 4 hours and stir every 30 minutes.

Enjoy your meal!

Coconut Ice Cream

Servings: 4
Cooking Time: 5 hours

INGREDIENTS:

- Cream 33% 400 ml
- Coconut milk 200 ml
- Sugar 150 g
- Egg yolk 3 pcs

DIRECTIONS:

1. Pour coconut milk into a saucepan, add sugar and yolks. Mix well with a whisk. We put the saucepan with the resulting mass in a water bath.
2. Cook over low heat, stirring constantly until thickened, 10 minutes. As soon as it begins to thicken, immediately remove so as not to turn into an omelet. The mass should look like condensed milk. Allow to cool completely.
3. Beat the cream with a mixer. Add chilled coconut custard to the whipped cream. We mix.
4. We transfer to a container and put in the freezer, stirring every 30 minutes 4-5 times.

Enjoy your meal!

Cherry Ice Cream

Servings: 3
Cooking Time: 9 hours

INGREDIENTS:

- Cherries 250 g pitted
- Cream 200 ml (30-33%)
- Condensed milk 150 g

DIRECTIONS:

1. Berries can be used both fresh and frozen. Refrigerate the cream for a better whipping.
2. Chop the cherries in a blender, add condensed milk and beat well again. Beat cold heavy cream with a mixer until smooth. Add whipped cream to the cherry and stir gently with a spatula until smooth. We put it in a container and put it in the freezer for 9 hours.
3. It is advisable to take out the ice cream and stir it every 30 minutes, that is, at least 5-6 times. After 5 hours, the mass does not need to be stirred.

Enjoy your meal!

Mint Ice Cream

Servings: 6
Cooking Time: 4 hours

INGREDIENTS:

- Cream - 400 ml (from 33% fat)
- Condensed milk - 200 ml
- Mint leaf - 30 g

DIRECTIONS:

1. Rinse the mint. For better whipping, the cream should be refrigerated for 1 hour.
2. Pour 200 ml of cream into a saucepan, add mint and bring to a boil. Remove from heat and cool for 2 hours. Then remove the mint from the cream and squeeze. Add 200 ml of cream and beat with a mixer until smooth. Then you need to mix the condensed milk with cream and mix well with a silicone spatula. We transfer to a container and put in the freezer overnight.

Enjoy your meal!

Watermelon Ice Cream

Servings: 6
Cooking Time: 4 hours

INGREDIENTS:

- Sliced watermelon 2 tbsp.
- Strawberries 2 tbsp.
- Milk 2 tbsp.
- Sugar 1 tbsp.
- Lime 1 tablespoon

DIRECTIONS:

1. Remove the seeds from the watermelon. Cut the strawberries in half. Place in a blender and pour over milk, add sugar and lime juice and chop well. Pour the resulting watermelon mass into a container and put in the freezer for 3 hours, remove and mix again in a blender and put in the freezer for another 1 hour.

Enjoy your meal!

Peach Ice Cream

Servings: 4
Cooking Time: 4 hours

INGREDIENTS:

- Chilled cream - 250 g (30-33% fat)
- Peach - 300 g
- Condensed milk - 80 g

DIRECTIONS:

1. Wash the peaches, remove the pit, cut into pieces and grind with a blender. Whip cold cream in a separate container until lightly thickened. Put the peach puree into the cream and mix well with a blender at low speed. Then pour in the condensed milk and mix well too. We put it in a container and put it in the freezer for 4 hours, I recommend stirring 2-3 times with an interval of 40 minutes.

   Enjoy your meal!

Apple Ice Cream

Servings: 6
Cooking Time: 12 hours

INGREDIENTS:

- Apple - 3-4 pieces
- Sugar - 1 tbsp.
- Milk - 2 tbsp.
- Salt - a pinch

DIRECTIONS:

1. Pour sugar, a pinch of salt into a saucepan and melt over low heat until caramel forms (10-15 minutes). Wash and peel the apples. Cut into pieces and chop in a blender. Then add the apples to the caramel and simmer until tender. Bring the milk to a boil and pour it into the apples in a thin stream while stirring. Allow to cool and rub through a sieve. We put it in a container and put it in the freezer for 12 hours.

   Enjoy your meal!

Grape Ice Cream

Servings: 6
Cooking Time: 4 hours

INGREDIENTS:

- Grapes - 3 tbsp
- Strawberries - ½ tbsp

DIRECTIONS:

1. Wash the grapes and remove the berries from the stem. Place in a blender, add strawberries and chop well on high speed. Pour the mixture into molds and insert wooden sticks. We put in the freezer for 12 hours.

   Enjoy your meal!

Plum Ice Cream

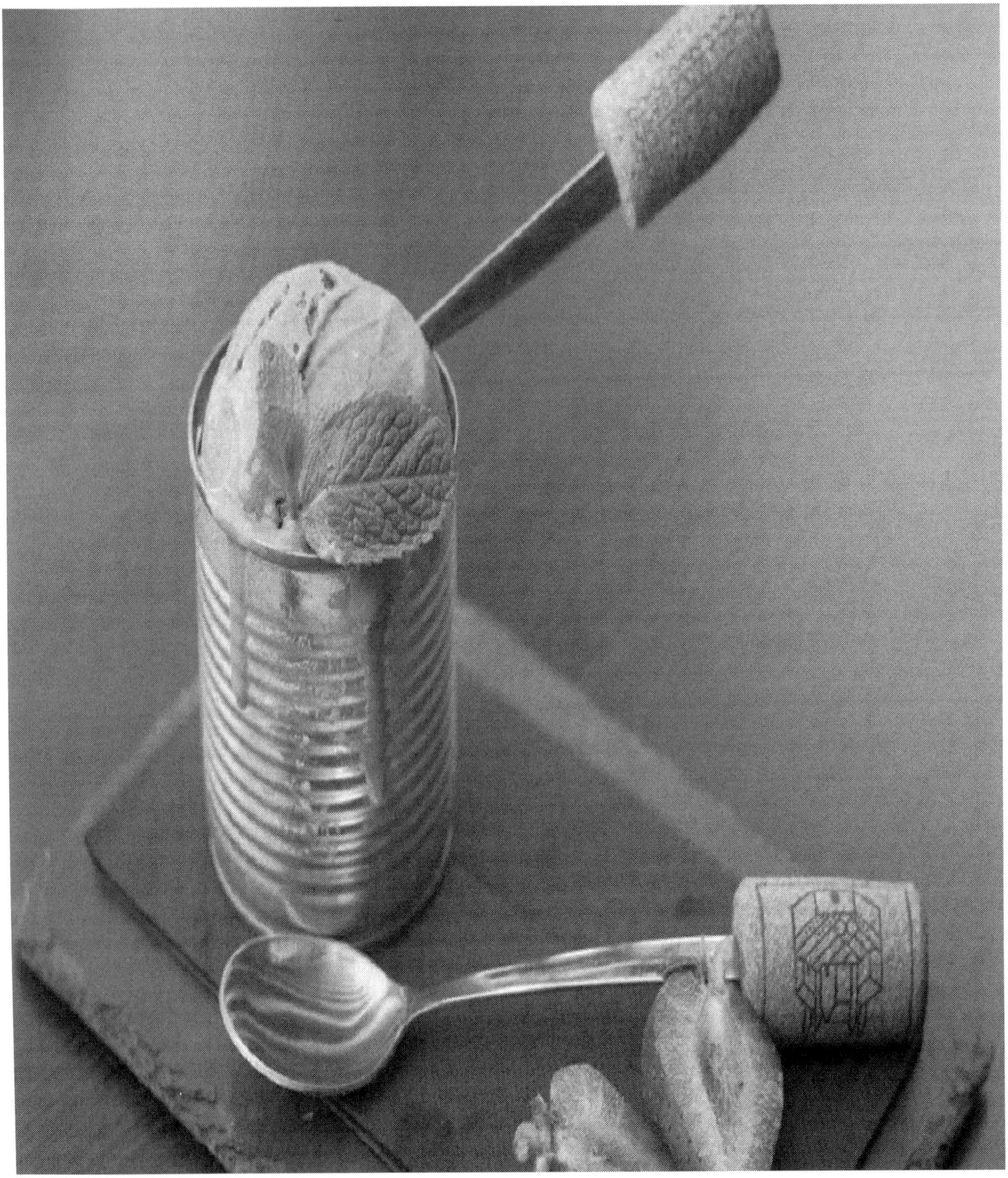

Servings: 6
Cooking Time: 4 hours

INGREDIENTS:

- Ripe plum 400 gr
- Sugar 1/2 tbsp
- Lemon juice 1 tbsp l
- Low-fat vanilla yogurt 2 tbsp

DIRECTIONS:

1. Wash the plums and remove the pit. Grind in a blender until smooth, then add sugar and lemon juice. Rub through a sieve. Add yogurt to the mixture and beat well with a blender. We put it in a container and put it in the freezer for 4 hours, stirring ice cream every 30 minutes.

Enjoy your meal!

Conclusion

I hope this book of recipes for delicious desserts such as sorbets and ice cream will bring you a very pleasant experience and an unforgettable aftertaste. You can make ice cream with children and it will bring even more joy to the whole family. Try, experiment and enjoy the process itself and you will see that you create your own masterpieces. Cook with pleasure and good mood.

Love Wendy Wood

Printed in Great Britain
by Amazon

83025091R00072